1 9 8 6

THE BOAT OF QUIET HOURS

The Boat
of Quiet Hours

POEMS BY JANE KENYON

GRAYWOLF PRESS · SAINT PAUL · MINNESOTA

ISBN 0-915308-86-x
ISBN 0-915308-87-8 (paperback)
Library of Congress Catalog Card Number 86-81787

First Printing, 1986
2 3 4 5 6 7 8 9

Cover art is "The Boat" by Claude Monet,
reproduced courtesy of Musée Marmottan

The type is Bembo
Typography by Tree Swenson
Manufactured by Arcata Graphics

Published by *GRAYWOLF PRESS*
Post Office Box 75006
Saint Paul, Minnesota 55175

ACKNOWLEDGMENTS

The author gratefully acknowledges the editors of the following periodicals, in which many of the poems in this collection first appeared.

American Poetry Review: Depression; Apple Dropping into Deep Early Snow.
Grand Street: Campers Leaving: 1981.
Harvard Magazine: Parents' Weekend: Camp Kenwood.
The Iowa Review: Briefly It Enters, and Briefly Speaks; Philosophy in Warm Weather; The Pond at Dusk; The Little Boat; The Sandy Hole; The Hermit; Sun and Moon; Deer Season; At the Summer Solstice.
Kenyon Review: At the Town Dump; Twilight: After Haying; Back from the City; Siesta: Barbados; Who.
The New Criterion: Alone for a Week; Drink, Eat, Sleep; High Water; The Painters; Sick at Summer's End; November Calf; The Visit; After Traveling; Siesta: Hotel Frattina.
New Letters: February: Thinking of Flowers.
The New Republic: Evening at a Country Inn; Things; The Appointment; Walking Alone in Late Winter; No Steps; Bright Sun After Heavy Snow; The Beaver Pool in December; Travel: After a Death.
The New Yorker: Song; Wash; Thinking of Madame Bovary.
Ploughshares: The Bat; Camp Evergreen; Mud Season; Photograph of a Child on a Vermont Hillside; Rain in January; Summer 1890: Near the Gulf; Frost Flowers; What Came to Me.
Poetry: Coming Home at Twilight in Late Summer; Evening Sun; Teacher; Inpatient; Whirligigs; Trouble with Math in a One-Room Country School; Inertia.
Seneca Review: Reading Late of the Death of Keats.
Virginia Quarterly Review: Main Street: Tilton, New Hampshire; Ice Storm; April Walk.

The author thanks the National Endowment for the Arts and the New Hampshire Commission on the Arts for support and encouragement during the writing of these poems.

And the author offers her deepest thanks to Donald Hall, Tess Gallagher, Joyce Peseroff, and Alice Mattison.

FOR PERKINS

TABLE OF CONTENTS

I. Walking Alone in Late Winter

II. Mud Season

III. The Boat of Quiet Hours

IV. Things

And, as the year
Grows lush in juicy stalks, I'll smoothly steer
My little boat, for many quiet hours,
With streams that deepen freshly into bowers.

JOHN KEATS
Endymion, Book I

I

Walking Alone in Late Winter

Evening at a Country Inn

From here I see a single red cloud
impaled on the Town Hall weathervane.
Now the horses are back in their stalls,
and the dogs are nowhere in sight
that made them run and buck
in the brittle morning light.

You laughed only once all day —
when the cat ate cucumbers
in Chekhov's story... and now you smoke
and pace the long hallway downstairs.

The cook is roasting meat for the evening meal,
and the smell rises to all the rooms.
Red-faced skiers stamp past you
on their way in; their hunger is Homeric.

I know you are thinking of the accident —
of picking the slivered glass from his hair.
Just now a truck loaded with hay
stopped at the village store to get gas.
I wish you would look at the hay —
the beautiful sane and solid bales of hay.

At the Town Dump

Sometimes I nod to my neighbor
as he flings lath and plaster or cleared
brush on the swelling pile. Talk
is impossible; the dozer shudders toward us,
flattening everything in its path.

Last March I got stuck in the mud.
Archie Portigue was there, thin
from the cancer that would kill him,
with his yellow pickup, its sides
akimbo from many loads. Archie
pushed as I rocked the car; the clutch
smelled hot; then with finesse
he jumped on the fender.... Saved,
I saw his small body in the rear-view mirror
get smaller as he waved.

A boy pokes with a stick at a burnt-out
sofa cushion.... He brings the insides
out with clear delight. Near where I stand
the toe of a boot protrudes from the sand.

Today I brought the bug-riddled remains
of my garden. A single ripe tomato — last fruit,
immaculate — evaded harvest, and dangles
from a vine. I offer it to oblivion
with the rest of what was mine.

Killing the Plants

That year I discovered the virtues
of plants as companions: they don't
argue, they don't ask for much,
they don't stay out until 3:00 A.M., then
lie to you about where they've been....

I can't summon the ambition
to repot this grape ivy, or this sad
old cactus, or even to move them out
onto the porch for the summer,
where their lives would certainly
improve. I give them
a grudging dash of water – that's all
they get. I wonder if they suspect

that like Hamlet I rehearse murder
all hours of the day and night,
considering the town dump
and compost pile as possible graves....

The truth is that if I permit them
to live, they will go on giving
alms to the poor: sweet air, miraculous
flowers, the example of persistence.

The Painters

A hot dry day in early fall....
The men have cut the vines
from the shutters, and scraped
the clapboards clean, and now
their heads appear all day
in all the windows...
their arms or shirtless torsos,
or a rainbow-speckled rag
swinging from a belt.

They work in earnest —
these are the last warm days.
Flies bump and buzz
between the screens and panes,
torpid from last night's frost:
the brittle months advance...
ruts frozen in the icy drive,
and the deeply black and soundless
nights. But now the painters

lean out from their ladders, squint
against the light, and lay on
the thick white paint.
From the lawn their radio predicts rain,
then cold Canadian air....
One of them works way up
on the dormer peak,
where a few wasps levitate
near the vestige of a nest.

Back from the City

After three days and nights of rich food
and late talk in overheated rooms,
of walks between mounds of garbage
and human forms bedded down for the night
under rags, I come back to my dooryard,
to my own wooden step.

The last red leaves fall to the ground
and frost has blackened the herbs and asters
that grew beside the porch. The air
is still and cool, and the withered grass
lies flat in the field. A nuthatch spirals
down the rough trunk of the tree.

At the Cloisters I indulged in piety
while gazing at a painted lindenwood Pietà —
Mary holding her pierced and desiccated son
across her knees; but when a man stepped close
under the tasseled awning of the hotel,
asking for "a quarter for someone
down on his luck," I quickly turned my back.

Now I hear tiny bits of bark and moss
break off under the bird's beak and claw,
and fall onto already-fallen leaves.
"Do you love me?" said Christ to his disciple.
"Lord, you know
that I love you."

                        "Then feed my sheep."

Deer Season

November, late afternoon. I'm driving fast,
only the parking lights on.
A minor infringement of the law....

All along Route 4 men wearing orange
step out of the woods after a day
of hunting, their rifles pointed
toward the ground.
                    The sky turns red, then
purple in the west, and the luminous
birches lean over the narrow macadam road.

I cross the little bridge
near the pool called The Pork Barrel,
where the best fishing is,
and pass the Fentons' farm — the windows
of the milking parlor bright, the great
silver cooling tank beginning to chill the milk.

I've seen the veal calves drink from pails
in their stalls. Suppose even the ear of wheat
suffers in the mill....
Moving fast in my car at dusk
I plan our evening meal.

November Calf

She calved in the ravine, beside
the green-scummed pond.
Full clouds and mist hung low —
it was unseasonably warm. Steam
rose from her head as she pushed
and called; her cries went out
over the still-lush fields.

First came the front feet, then
the blossom-nose, shell-pink
and glistening; and then the broad
forehead, flopping black ears,
and neck.... She worked
until the steaming length of him
rushed out onto the ground, then
turned and licked him with her wide
pink tongue. He lifted up his head
and looked around.

The herd pressed close to see, then
frolicked up the bank, flicking
their tails. It looked like revelry.
The farmer set off for the barn,
swinging in a widening arc
a frayed and knotted scrap of rope.

The Beaver Pool in December

The brook is still open
where the water falls,
but over the deeper pools
clear ice forms; over the dark
shapes of stones, a rotting log,
and amber leaves that clattered down
after the first heavy frost.

Though I wait in the cold
until dusk, and though a sudden
bubble of air rises under the ice,
I see not a single animal.

The beavers thrive somewhere
else, eating the bark of hoarded
saplings. How they struggled
to pull the long branches
over the stiffening bank...

but now they pass without
effort, all through the chilly
water; moving like thoughts
in an unconflicted mind.

Apple Dropping into Deep Early Snow

A jay settled on a branch, making it sway.
The one shriveled fruit that remained
gave way to the deepening drift below.
I happened to see it the moment it fell.

Dusk is eager and comes early. A car
creeps over the hill. Still in the dark I try
to tell if I am numbered with the damned,
who cry, outraged, *Lord, when did we see You?*

Drink, Eat, Sleep

I never drink from this blue tin cup
speckled with white
without thinking of stars on a clear,
cold night — of Venus blazing low
over the leafless trees; and Canis
great and small — dogs without flesh,
fur, blood, or bone... dogs made of light,
apparitions of cold light, with black
and trackless spaces in between....
The angel gave a little book
to the prophet, telling him to eat —
eat and tell of the end of time.
Strange food, infinitely strange,
but the pages were like honey
to his tongue....

Rain in January

I woke before dawn, still
in a body. Water ran
down every window, and rushed
from the eaves.

Beneath the empty feeder
a skunk was prowling for suet
or seed. The lamps flickered off
and then came on again.

Smoke from the chimney
could not rise. It came down
into the yard, and brooded there
on the unlikelihood of reaching

heaven. When my arm slipped
from the arm of the chair
I let it hang beside me, pale,
useless, and strange.

Depression in Winter

There comes a little space between the south
side of a boulder
and the snow that fills the woods around it.
Sun heats the stone, reveals
a crescent of bare ground: brown ferns,
and tufts of needles like red hair,
acorns, a patch of moss, bright green....

I sank with every step up to my knees,
throwing myself forward with a violence
of effort, greedy for unhappiness —
until by accident I found the stone,
with its secret porch of heat and light,
where something small could luxuriate, then
turned back down my path, chastened and calm.

Bright Sun after Heavy Snow

A ledge of ice slides from the eaves,
piercing the crusted drift. Astonishing
how even a little violence
eases the mind.

In this extreme state of light
everything seems flawed: the streaked
pane, the forced bulbs on the sill
that refuse to bloom.... A wad of dust
rolls like a desert weed
over the drafty floor.

Again I recall a neighbor's
small affront — it rises in my mind
like the huge banks of snow along the road:
the plow, passing up and down all day,
pushes them higher and higher....

The shadow of smoke rising from the chimney
moves abruptly over the yard.
The clothesline rises in the wind. One
wooden pin is left, solitary as a finger;
it, too, rises and falls.

Ice Storm

For the hemlocks and broad-leafed evergreens
a beautiful and precarious state of being....
Here in the suburbs of New Haven
nature, unrestrained, lops the weaker limbs
of shrubs and trees with a sense of æsthetics
that is practical and sinister....

I am a guest in this house.
On the bedside table *Good Housekeeping*, and
A Nietzsche Reader.... The others are still asleep.
The most painful longing comes over me.
A longing not of the body...

It could be for beauty —
I mean what Keats was panting after,
for which I love and honor him;
it could be for the promises of God;
or for oblivion, *nada*; or some condition even more
extreme, which I intuit, but can't quite name.

Walking Alone in Late Winter

How long the winter has lasted — like a Mahler
symphony, or an hour in the dentist's chair.
In the fields the grasses are matted
and gray, making me think of June, when hay
and vetch burgeon in the heat, and warm rain
swells the globed buds of the peony.

Ice on the pond breaks into huge planes. One
sticks like a barge gone awry at the neck
of the bridge.... The reeds
and shrubby brush along the shore
gleam with ice that shatters when the breeze
moves them. From beyond the bog
the sound of water rushing over trees
felled by the zealous beavers,
who bring them crashing down.... Sometimes
it seems they do it just for fun.

Those days of anger and remorse
come back to me; you fidgeting with your ring,
sliding it off, then jabbing it on again.

The wind is keen coming over the ice;
it carries the sound of breaking glass.
And the sun, bright but not warm,
has gone behind the hill. Chill, or the fear
of chill, sends me hurrying home.

II

Mud Season

The Hermit

The meeting ran needlessly late,
and while yawns were suppressed around the room
the river swelled until it spilled.
When the speaker finished, I made for the car
and home as fast as fog would allow —
until I came upon a barricade: beyond,
black pools eddied over the road. Detour.
The last familiar thing I saw: the steaming
heaps of bark beside the lumber mill.

No other cars on the narrow, icy lane; no house
or barn for miles, until the lights of a Christmas tree
shone from the small windows of a trailer.
And then I knew I couldn't be far
from the East Village and the main road.
I was terribly wide awake....

To calm myself I thought of drinking water
at the kitchen sink, in the circle of light
the little red lamp makes in the evening...
of half-filling a second glass
and splashing it into the dish of white narcissus
growing on the sill. In China
this flower is called the hermit,
and people greet the turning of the year
with bowls of freshly opened blossoms....

The Pond at Dusk

A fly wounds the water but the wound
soon heals. Swallows tilt and twitter
overhead, dropping now and then toward
the outward-radiating evidence of food.

The green haze on the trees changes
into leaves, and what looks like smoke
floating over the neighbor's barn
is only apple blossoms.

But sometimes what looks like disaster
is disaster: the day comes at last,
and the men struggle with the casket
just clearing the pews.

High Water

Eight days of rain;
the ground refuses more.
My neighbors are morose at the village store.

I'm sick of holding still, sick of indoors,
so I walk through the heavy-headed grasses
to watch the river reach
for the bridge's wooden planks,
bending the lithe swamp maples
that grow along the banks.

Nothing but trouble comes to mind
as I lean over the rusty iron rail.
I know of plenty, in detail, that is not
my own. I nudge a pebble over the edge.
It drops with a *thunk* into the water —
dark, voluminous, and clear,
and moving headlong away from here.

Evening Sun

Why does this light force me back
to my childhood? I wore a yellow
summer dress, and the skirt
made a perfect circle.

                Turning and turning
until it flared to the limit
was irresistible.... The grass and trees,
my outstretched arms, and the skirt
whirled in the ochre light
of an early June evening.

                  And I knew then
that I would have to live, and go on
living: what a sorrow it was; and still
what sorrow burns
but does not destroy my heart.

Summer 1890: Near the Gulf

The hour was late, and the others
were asleep. He struck a match
on the wooden railing of the porch
and lit a cigarette

while she beheld his head and hand,
estranged from the body
in wavering light....

What she felt then
would, like heavy wind
and rain, bring
any open flower to the ground.

He let the spent match
fall; but the face remained
before her, like a bright light
before a closed eye....

Photograph of a Child on a Vermont Hillside

Beside the rocking horse, for which
she has grown too large,
and the shirts that hang still on the line,
she looks down.
The face is dour and pale
with something private, and will not admit
the journalist, up from Boston
for country color.

How well she knows these hills —
green receding unaccountably to blue —
and the low meadow in middle distance,
buff-colored now, with one
misshapen tree. . . .

What would she say if she cared
to speak a word? a word meaning
childhood is woe in solitude,
and the bliss of turning circles
barefoot in the dusty drive
after the supper dishes are done. . . .

What Came to Me

I took the last
dusty piece of china
out of the barrel.
It was your gravy boat,
with a hard, brown
drop of gravy still
on the porcelain lip.
I grieved for you then
as I never had before.

Main Street: Tilton, New Hampshire

I waited in the car while he
went into the small old-fashioned grocery
for a wedge of cheddar.

Late summer, Friday afternoon.
A mother and child walked past
trading mock blows
with paper bags full of — what —
maybe new clothes for school.
They turned the corner by the laundromat,
and finally even the heel
of the girl's rubber flip-flop
passed from sight.

Across the street a blue pickup, noisy,
with some kind of home-made wooden
scaffolding in the bed, pulled
close to the curb. A man got out
and entered the bank....
                                        A woman sat
in the cab, dabbing her face
with a tissue. She might have been weeping,
but it was hot and still,
and maybe she wasn't weeping at all.

Through time and space we came
to Main Street — three days before
Labor Day, 1984, 4:47 in the afternoon;
and then that moment passed, displaced
by others equally equivocal.

Teacher

Sometimes there's gravel on the bend
by Vernondale's Store in North Sutton.
I've learned to watch for that,
and for the German Shepherd
who lies in the road
at the foot of his master's drive.

I've seen the farm market signs
change with the weather: *Potatoes,*
to *Pumpkins,* to *Firewood: Inquire Within.*

My students have stayed the same.
They still cut class to go skiing
or fix their cars,
and they continue to write:
. . . his flowing mane and proud bearing
are timeless symbols of the pure blood
coursing through his royal veins. . . .

Today the marsh is white with ice.
The reeds look brittle and defeated.
While I was at work
someone covered the three poplars
by that cottage porch; wrapped them
in canvas against ice and wind,
then cinched the canvas with ropes,
making waists for the three lithe caryatids,
who seem to be holding up the roof
while they wait for April thaw. . . .

Frost Flowers

Sap withdraws from the upper reaches
of maples; the squirrel digs deeper
and deeper in the moss
to bury the acorns that fall
all around, distracting him.

I'm out here in the dusk,
tired from teaching and a little drunk,
where the wild asters, last blossoms
of the season, straggle uphill.
Frost flowers, I've heard them called.
The white ones have yellow centers
at first: later they darken
to a rosy copper. They're mostly done.
Then the blue ones come on. It's blue
all around me now, though the color
has gone with the sun.

My sarcasm wounded a student today.
Afterward I heard him running down the stairs.

There is no one at home but me —
and I'm not at home; I'm up here on the hill,
looking at the dark windows below.
Let them be dark. Some large bird
calls down-mountain — a cry
astonishingly loud, distressing....

I was cruel to him: it is a bitter thing.
The air is damp and cold,
and by now I am a little hungry....
The squirrel is high in the oak,
gone to his nest, and night has silenced
the last loud rupture of the calm.

The Sandy Hole

The infant's coffin no bigger than a flightbag....
The young father steps backward from the sandy hole,
eyes wide and dry, his hand over his mouth.
No one dares to come near him, even to touch his sleeve.

Depression

...a mote. A little world. Dusty. Dusty.
The universe is dust. Who can bear it?
Christ comes. The women feed him, bathe his feet
with tears, bring spices, find the empty tomb,
burst out to tell the men, are not believed....

Sun and Moon

FOR DONALD CLARK

Drugged and drowsy but not asleep
I heard my blind roommate's daughter
helping her with her meal:
"What's that? Squash?"
"No. It's spinach."

Back from a brain-scan, she dozed
to the sound of the Soaps: adultery,
amnesia, shady business deals,
and long, white hospital halls. . . .
No separation between life and art.

I heard two nurses whispering:
Mr. Malcomson had died.
An hour later one of them came to say
that a private room was free.

A chill spring breeze
perturbed the plastic drape.
I lay back on the new bed,
and had a vision of souls
stacked up like pelts
under my soul, which was ill —
so heavy with grief
it kept the others from rising.

No varicolored tubes
serpentined beneath the covers;
I had the vital signs of a healthy,
early-middle-aged woman.
There was nothing to cut or dress,
remove or replace.

43

A week of stupor. Sun and moon
rose and set over the small enclosed
court, the trees. . . .
The doctor's face appeared
and disappeared
over the foot of the bed. By slow degrees
the outlandish sadness waned.

Restored to my living room
I looked at the tables, chairs, and pictures
with something like delight,
only pale, faint — as from a great height.
I let the phone ring; the mail
accrued unopened
on the table in the hall.

Whirligigs

Two bearded men: one chops a log,
the other milks a cow. Even at night
they turn their backsides to the strongest
gusts and work like mad, but never
finish, though they bend over the same log
and the same cow for the third year
in a row.
        They winter in the cellar,
near the apple cider kegs. For all I know
they take a nip or two, pass stories back
and forth with a speckled tinware cup.

Come spring I reinstate them
on weathered poles among the scilla
and early daffodils. I think they must be
brothers... and we three make a family,
waving our arms to scare the crows away.

February: Thinking of Flowers

Now wind torments the field,
turning the white surface back
on itself, back and back on itself,
like an animal licking a wound.

Nothing but white — the air, the light;
only one brown milkweed pod
bobbing in the gully, smallest
brown boat on the immense tide.

A single green sprouting thing
would restore me....

Then think of the tall delphinium,
swaying, or the bee when it comes
to the tongue of the burgundy lily.

Portrait of a Figure near Water

Rebuked, she turned and ran
uphill to the barn. Anger, the inner
arsonist, held a match to her brain.
She observed her life: against her will
it survived the unwavering flame.

The barn was empty of animals.
Only a swallow tilted
near the beams, and bats
hung from the rafters
the roof sagged between.

Her breath became steady
where, years past, the farmer cooled
the big tin amphoræ of milk.
The stone trough was still
filled with water: she watched it
and received its calm.

So it is when we retreat in anger:
we think we burn alone
and there is no balm.
Then water enters, though it makes
no sound.

Mud Season

Here in purgatory bare ground
is visible, except in shady places
where snow prevails.

Still, each day sees
the restoration of another animal:
a sparrow, just now a sleepy wasp;
and, at twilight, the skunk
pokes out of the den,
anxious for mates and meals....

On the floor of the woodshed
the coldest imaginable ooze,
and soon the first shoots
of asparagus will rise,
the fingers of Lazarus....

Earth's open wounds — where the plow
gouged the ground last November —
must be smoothed; some sown
with seed, and all forgotten.

Now the nuthatch spurns the suet,
resuming its diet of flies, and the mesh
bag, limp and greasy, might be taken
down.

Beside the porch step
the crocus prepares an exaltation
of purple, but for the moment
holds its tongue....

III

The Boat of Quiet Hours

Thinking of Madame Bovary

The first hot April day the granite step
was warm. Flies droned in the grass.
When a car went past they rose
in unison, then dropped back down....

I saw that a yellow crocus bud had pierced
a dead oak leaf, then opened wide. How strong
its appetite for the luxury of the sun!

Everyone longs for love's tense joys and red delights.

And then I spied an ant
dragging a ragged, disembodied wing
up the warm brick walk. It must have been
the Methodist in me that leaned forward,
preceded by my shadow, to put a twig just where
the ant was struggling with its own desire.

April Walk

Evening came, and work was done.
We went for a walk to see
what winter had exacted
from our swimming place on the pond.

The moss was immoderately green,
and spongy underfoot; stepping on it seemed
a breach of etiquette.
We found our picnic table
sitting squarely in the bog — only
a minor prank. The slender birches watched us
leaning from the bank.

And where the river launches forth
from the south end of the pond
the water coursed high and clear
under the little bridge.
Huge, suspended in the surge, grand–
father turtle moved sporadically
one flat, prehistoric, clawed arm
at a time, keeping his head downstream.

Years ago he made a vow
not to be agitated by the runnels
of spring, the abundance of light,
warm wind smelling of rain,
or the peepers' throstling. . . .

We watched till he was out of sight
and seemed illusory, then turned
toward home — the windows
brazen in the setting sun. . . .

Philosophy in Warm Weather

Now all the doors and windows
are open, and we move so easily
through the rooms. Cats roll
on the sunny rugs, and a clumsy wasp
climbs the pane, pausing
to rub a leg over her head.

All around physical life reconvenes.
The molecules of our bodies must love
to exist: they whirl in circles
and seem to begrudge us nothing.
Heat, Horatio, *heat* makes them
put this antic disposition on!

This year's brown spider
sways over the door as I come
and go. A single poppy shouts
from the far field, and the crow,
beyond alarm, goes right on
pulling up the corn.

No Steps

The young bull dropped his head and stared.
Only a wispy wire – electrified – kept us
apart. That, and two long rows of asparagus.
An ancient apple tree
blossomed prodigally pink and white.

The muddy path sucked at my shoe,
but I reached the granite step, and knocked
at the rickety porch door.
Deep in the house a dog began to bark.
I had prepared my Heart Fund speech,
and the first word – *When* – was on my tongue.

I heard no steps – only the breeze
riffling the tender poplar leaves,
and a random, meditative *moo*
behind me.... Relieved, I turned back
to the car, passing once more
under the bull's judicial eye....
Everything was intact: the canister,
still far too light and mute,
and metal boutonnières where they began –
in a zip-lock plastic sandwich bag.

Wash

All day the blanket snapped and swelled
on the line, roused by a hot spring wind....
From there it witnessed the first sparrow,
early flies lifting their sticky feet,
and a green haze on the south-sloping hills.
Clouds rode over the mountain.... At dusk
I took the blanket in, and we slept,
restless, under its fragrant weight.

Inertia

My head was heavy, heavy;
so was the atmosphere.
I had to ask two times
before my hand would scratch my ear.
I thought I should be out
and doing! The grass, for one thing,
needed mowing.

Just then a centipede
reared from the spine
of my open dictionary. It tried
the air with enterprising feelers,
then made its way along the gorge
between 202 and 203. *The valley
of the shadow of death* came to mind
inexorably.

It can't be easy for the left hand
to know what the right is doing.
And how, on such a day, when the sky
is hazy and perfunctory, how does it
get itself started without feeling
muddled and heavy-hearted?

Well, it had its fill of etymology.
I watched it pull its tail
over the edge of the page, and vanish
in a pile of mail.

Camp Evergreen

The boats like huge bright birds
sail back when someone calls them:
the small campers struggle out
and climb the hill to lunch.
I see the last dawdler
disappear in a ridge of trees.

The whole valley sighs
in the haze and heat of noon. Far out
a fish astonishes the air, falls back
into its element. From the marshy cove
the bullfrog offers thoughts
on the proper limits of ambition.

An hour passes. Piano music
comes floating over the water, falters,
begins again, falters....
Only work will make it right.

Some small thing I can't quite see
clatters down through the leafy dome.
Now it is high summer: the solstice:
longed-for, possessed, luxurious, and sad.

The Appointment

The phoebe flew back and forth
between the fencepost and the tree —
not nest-building, just restlessly...
and I heard the motorboat on the lake,
going around and through its own wake,
towing the campers two by two.

I thought of a dozen things to do
but rejected them all
in favor of fretting about you.
It might have been the finest day of summer —
the hay was rich and dry, and the breeze
made the heart-shaped leaves of the birch
tell all their secrets,
though they were lost on me....

Bees rummaged through the lilies, methodical
as thieves in a chest of drawers.
I saw them from the chair
nearest the cool foundation stones.
Out of the cellar window came
a draught of damp and evil-smelling air.

The potted geraniums on the porch
hung limp in the blaze of noon. I could
not stir to water them. If you
had turned into the drive just then, even
with cheerful news, I doubt
I could have heard what you had to say.

Sick at Summer's End

Today from the darkened room I heard
the men across the lake, taking up the dock
for winter. They stacked the clattering sections
well up the sandy slope, then
shedded the canoes; I suppose
they left the cabins locked.

Late afternoon the paper carrier's car
slowed on the blacktop, stopped,
and, flinging gravel, started up again.

I know the garden ramps and goes
to seed. And the blue jay chills
with its call that sounds like the butcher's
saw when it cuts into bone.
The room turns darker still
by insensible degrees, and crickets
shrill from the window well....

I'm falling upward, nothing to hold me down.

Alone for a Week

I washed a load of clothes
and hung them out to dry.
Then I went up to town
and busied myself all day.
The sleeve of your best shirt
rose ceremonious
when I drove in; our night-
clothes twined and untwined in
a little gust of wind.

For me it was getting late;
for you, where you were, not.
The harvest moon was full
but sparse clouds made its light
not quite reliable.
The bed on your side seemed
as wide and flat as Kansas;
your pillow plump, cool,
and allegorical....

The Bat

I was reading about rationalism,
the kind of thing we do up north
in early winter, where the sun
leaves work for the day at 4:15.

Maybe the world *is* intelligible
to the rational mind;
and maybe we light the lamps at dusk
for nothing. . . .

Then I heard wings overhead.

The cats and I chased the bat
in circles — living room, kitchen,
pantry, kitchen, living room. . . .
At every turn it evaded us

like the identity of the third person
in the Trinity: the one
who spoke through the prophets,
the one who astounded Mary
by suddenly coming near.

Siesta: Barbados

From bed we heard
the gardener move down the hedge
of oleander, chopping out the weeds
with her long, curved cutlass
and singing. A lizard gripped the coarse
stucco of the ceiling. It pulsed;
it cocked its head; and when the blade
rang out against a stone
it flicked its question-mark of a tail
around to the other side....
Sea breeze swelled the curtain,
and tried the shuttered door...
and then you reached for the hem
of my red dress with blue leaves
and lemon lilies – the one you bought for me
from the woman who came to our porch
balancing a bundle on her head.

Trouble with Math in a One-Room Country School

The others bent their heads and started in.
Confused, I asked my neighbor
to explain — a sturdy, bright-cheeked girl
who brought raw milk to school from her family's
herd of Holsteins. Ann had a blue bookmark,
and on it Christ revealed his beating heart,
holding the flesh back with His wounded hand.
Ann understood division....

Miss Moran sprang from her monumental desk
and led me roughly through the class
without a word. My shame was radical
as she propelled me past the cloakroom
to the furnace closet, where only the boys
were put, only the older ones at that.
The door swung briskly shut.

The warmth, the gloom, the smell
of sweeping compound clinging to the broom
soothed me. I found a bucket, turned it
upside down, and sat, hugging my knees.
I hummed a theme from Haydn that I knew
from my piano lessons...
and hardened my heart against authority.
And then I heard her steps, her fingers
on the latch. She led me, blinking
and changed, back to the class.

The Little Boat

As soon as spring peepers sounded from the stream
and boggy lower barnyard across the road
Mother let us bring out the cots,
and sleeping bags — red and gray and black
plaid flannel, still smelling of the cedar chest.

How hard it was to settle down that first night
out on the big screened porch: three times
trains passed the crossing, and the peepers' song
was lost under the whistle (two long,
two short), the rumble and clacking,
and clang of the crossing bell. The neighbor's
cocker spaniel howled the whole time
and for a full two minutes after.... Or rain
sluiced from the eaves, and we saw black limbs
against a sky whitened by lightning.
The gloom was lavish and agreeable....

August came. Mother took us to Wahr's on State Street,
bought each of us a reader, speller, Big 10 Tablet,
a bottle of amber glue with a slit like a closed eye,
pencils, erasers of a violent pink, a penmanship workbook
for practicing loops that looked to me
like the culvert under the road, whose dark and webby length
Brother and I dared each other to run through...
and crayons, the colors ranging from one to another
until what began as yellow ended amazingly as blue.

One morning we walked to the top of Foster Road,
and stood under the Reimers' big maple.
Ground fog rose from the hay stubble.
We heard gears grinding at the foot of the hill;
the bus appeared and we knew we had to get in.

All day in my imagination my body floated
above the classroom, navigating easily
between fluorescent shoals.... I was listening,
floating, watching.... The others stayed below
at their desks (I saw the crown of my own head
bending over a book), and no one knew I was not
where I seemed to be....

IV

Things

Song

An oriole sings from the hedge
and in the hotel kitchen
the chef sweetens cream for pastries.
Far off, lightning and thunder agree
to join us for a few days
here in the valley. How lucky we are
to be holding hands on a porch
in the country. But even this
is not the joy that trembles
under every leaf and tongue.

At the Summer Solstice

Noon heat. And later, hotter still....
The neighbor's son rides up and down the field
turning the hay — turning it with flourishes.

The tractor dips into the low clovery place
where melt from the mountain
comes down in the spring, and wild
lupine grows. Only the boy's blond head
can be seen; but then he comes smartly
up again — to whirl, deft, around
the pear tree near the barn. Bravo...

bravissimo. The tall grass lies — cut,
turned, raked, and dry. Later his father
comes down the lane with the baler. I hear
the steady thumping all afternoon.

So hot, so hot today.... I will stay in our room
with the shades drawn, waiting for you
to come with sleepy eyes, and pass your fingers
lightly, lightly up my thighs.

Coming Home at Twilight in Late Summer

We turned into the drive,
and gravel flew up from the tires
like sparks from a fire. So much
to be done — the unpacking, the mail
and papers...the grass needed mowing....
We climbed stiffly out of the car.
The shut-off engine ticked as it cooled.

And then we noticed the pear tree,
the limbs so heavy with fruit
they nearly touched the ground.
We went out to the meadow; our steps
made black holes in the grass;
and we each took a pear,
and ate, and were grateful.

The Visit

The talkative guest has gone,
and we sit in the yard
saying nothing. The slender moon
comes over the peak of the barn.

The air is damp, and dense
with the scent of honeysuckle....
The last clever story has been told
and answered with laughter.

With my sleeping self I met
my obligations, but now I am aware
of the silence, and your affection,
and the delicate sadness of dusk.

Parents' Weekend: Camp Kenwood

Mid-morning the company of cars
began to cross the little bridge;
the loose plank knocked and knocked.
The dog established her front feet
on the fence and barked.

Now the *pock-pick-pock* of tennis
floats over the lake, and the slap
of the ball when it hits the tape...
or children's voices singing
and prolonged applause. The breeze

comes from the south, is seasonably warm,
exciting the water to a bright confusion.
Once we set off for the woods
with little silver berry pails; then
everything seemed right just as it was....

Reading Late of the Death of Keats

I tried to distract myself by reading
late, but the rhythmic whirr and puff
of the oxygen machine reached me
where I lay, in the room
that was mine in childhood.

Clearly I had packed the wrong book
in my haste: Keats died, propped up
to get more air. Severn
straightened the body on the bed,
and cut three dampened curls
from Keats's head.

A huge moth bumped against the screen,
tattering its wings. I turned
off the lamp and lay, all ears,
until it flew or fell away. . . .

Inpatient

The young attendants wrapped him in a red
velour blanket, and pulled the strapping taut.
Sedated on the stretcher and outside
for the last time, he raised his head and sniffed
the air like an animal. A wedge of geese
flew honking over us. The sky leaned close;
a drop of rain fell on his upturned face.
I stood aside, steward of Grandma's red–
letter New Testament and an empty vase.
The nurse went with him through the sliding door.
Without having to speak of it we left
the suitcase with his streetclothes in the car.

Campers Leaving: Summer 1981

Just now two chartered buses from Boston
pulled majestically onto Route 4. Dust
settled along the back road...the dog
stopped barking, turned three circles,
and lay back down.

Faces in every tinted window
turned back for one last look
at Ragged Mountain.
The sun had cleared the peak...
it was so bright they had to turn away. Soon
the noisy reconstruction of every family....

Yesterday the phone rang at noon.
Father, calling from the hospital, had
something on his irradiated mind — just what,
he couldn't say, not that he didn't try.
He wept, and gave the phone to Mother
to say good-bye.

All summer I watched the campers from the far
shore. They learned to swim and sail,
and how to cling to a tipped canoe. Some
struggled the entire time but failed.
On the last day I heard a voice
say simply, *I need the pole.*
Sometimes when the wind is right it seems
that every word has been spoken to me.

Travel: After a Death

We drove past farms, the hills terraced with sheep.
A rook flapped upward from the stubbled corn:
its shadow fell across my lap one instant
and then was gone. The car was warm. Sleepy,
we passed through Devonshire: sun and showers....
Fields, emerald in January, shone
through leafless hedges, and I watched a man
grasping his plaid cloth cap and walking stick
in one hand, while with perfect courtesy
he sent his dog before him through the stile,
bowing a little like a maître d'.

We found a room in a cold seaside hotel.
The manager had left a sullen girl
— no more than eighteen — and a parakeet
to run his business while he sunned himself
in Portugal. We watched her rip the key
from the wall and fling it toward us. Why,
I wondered, was the front door wedged open
in January, with a raw sea wind
blowing the woolen skirts of the townswomen,
who passed with market baskets on their arms,
their bodies bent forward against the chill
and the steep angle of the cobbled hill?

There were two urns of painted porcelain
flanking the door. A man could stand in one
and still have room for ashes...though he'd have
to be a strange man, like the poet Donne,
who pulled a shroud around himself and called
someone to draw — from life — his deathbed scene;
or like Turgenev, who saw bones and skulls
instead of Londoners walking the streets....
Oh, when am I going to own my mind again?

77

Yard Sale

Under the stupefying sun
my family's belongings lie on the lawn
or heaped on borrowed card tables
in the gloom of the garage. Platters,
frying pans, our dead dog's
dish, box upon box of sheet music,
a wad of my father's pure linen
hand-rolled handkerchiefs, and his books
on the subsistence farm, a dream
for which his constitution ill suited him.

My niece dips seashells
in a glass of Coke. Sand streaks giddily
between bubbles to the bottom. Brown runnels
seem to scar her arm. "Do something silly!"
she begs her aunt. Listless,
I put a lampshade on my head.
Not good enough.

My brother takes pity on her
and they go walking together along the river
in places that seemed numinous
when we were five and held hands
with our young parents.
                              She comes back
triumphant, with a plastic pellet box the size
of a bar of soap, which her father has clipped
to the pouch of her denim overalls. In it,
a snail with a slate-blue shell, and a few
blades of grass to make it feel at home....

Hours pass. We close the metal strongbox
and sit down, stunned by divestiture.
What would he say? My niece
produces drawings and hands them over shyly:

a house with flowers, family
standing shoulder to shoulder
near the door under an affable sun,
and one she calls "Ghost with Long Legs."

Siesta: Hotel Frattina

Mid-afternoon the sound of weeping in the hall
woke me... hurried steps on the stair, and a door
slamming. I put on my glasses and stared
at nothing in particular.

We had walked all morning in the Forum
among pillars, cornices, and tilting
marble floors... armless torsos, faces
missing their noses — all fallen awry
among the grassy knolls.

Lord Byron brooded there on his love
for Teresa Guiccioli, only nineteen,
and someone else's wife. Oh, Siren Italy.

Just then the faucet gasped.
The ceiling seemed incalculably far away.
My mind revolted at all I had bought
in the chic little alleyways of Rome.

I longed for home, and the high collars we wear
a hundred miles north of the place
where Hawthorne wrote *The Scarlet Letter.*

I even longed to be bored again,
watching the pale sun rush — all business —
over the edge of the western world
by four on a November afternoon.

After Traveling

While in silence I rake
my plot of grass under the great trees —
the oaks and monumental maples —
I think of the proprietor

of the Caffè dei Fiori, sleepy, preoccupied,
dressed to the nines,
setting out tables in the Via Frattina —
extending his empire each day
by the smallest of increments
until there is room for another place...

at which we happen to be sitting
on the day the city official comes,
also dressed to the nines, to unwind
his shining metal measure in the street:
two tables must go. But for now
the proprietor shrugs, and a look
of infinite weariness passes
over his face. This is Rome:
remorse would be anomalous....

And the white-coated waiters
arrange on doilied silver trays
the tiers of sugared pastries: angel wings,
cat tongues, and little kiwi tarts;
and the coffee machines fizzle and spurt
such appetizing steam; and a woman
in a long red cape goes by
leading a matched pair of pugs
on a bifurcated leash.

Twilight: After Haying

Yes, long shadows go out
from the bales; and yes, the soul
must part from the body:
what else could it do?

The men sprawl near the baler,
reluctant to leave the field.
They talk and smoke,
and the tips of their cigarettes
blaze like small roses
in the night air. (It arrived
and settled among them
before they were aware.)

The moon comes
to count the bales,
and the dispossessed —
Whip-poor-will, Whip-poor-will
— sings from the dusty stubble.

These things happen...the soul's bliss
and suffering are bound together
like the grasses....

The last, sweet exhalations
of timothy and vetch
go out with the song of the bird;
the ravaged field
grows wet with dew.

Who

These lines are written
by an animal, an angel,
a stranger sitting in my chair;
by someone who already knows
how to live without trouble
among books, and pots and pans....

Who is it who asks me to find
language for the sound
a sheep's hoof makes when it strikes
a stone? And who speaks
the words which are my food?

Briefly It Enters, and Briefly Speaks

I am the blossom pressed in a book,
found again after two hundred years....

I am the maker, the lover, and the keeper....

When the young girl who starves
sits down to a table
she will sit beside me....

I am food on the prisoner's plate....

I am water rushing to the well-head,
filling the pitcher until it spills....

I am the patient gardener
of the dry and weedy garden....

I am the stone step,
the latch, and the working hinge....

I am the heart contracted by joy...
the longest hair, white
before the rest....

I am there in the basket of fruit
presented to the widow....

I am the musk rose opening
unattended, the fern on the boggy summit....

I am the one whose love
overcomes you, already with you
when you think to call my name....

Things

The hen flings a single pebble aside
with her yellow, reptilian foot.
Never in eternity the same sound —
a small stone falling on a red leaf.

The juncture of twig and branch,
scarred with lichen, is a gate
we might enter, singing.

The mouse pulls batting
from a hundred-year-old quilt.
She chewed a hole in a blue star
to get it, and now she thrives....
Now is her time to thrive.

Things: simply lasting, then
failing to last: water, a blue heron's
eye, and the light passing
between them: into light all things
must fall, glad at last to have fallen.

JANE KENYON was born in Ann Arbor and graduated from the University of Michigan. Her poems have appeared in many magazines including *The New Yorker*, *The Paris Review*, and *The New Republic*. She is the author of *From Room to Room* (Alice James Books, 1978) and *Twenty Poems of Anna Akhmatova* (Ally/The Eighties Press, 1985). She and her husband, Donald Hall, live and work in Wilmot, New Hampshire.